GRANDMA'S
WIT AND WISDOM

QUIPS AND QUOTES FOR THE GREATEST GRANNIES

RICHARD BENSON

summersdale

GRANDMA'S WIT AND WISDOM

Copyright © Summersdale Publishers Ltd, 2017

Research by Katherine Kingsford

Summersdale Publishers Ltd
46 West Street
Chichester
West Sussex
PO19 1RP
UK

www.summersdale.com

Printed and bound in the Czech Republic

ISBN: 978-1-78685-063-8

Substantial discounts on bulk quantities of Summersdale books are available to corporations, professional associations and other organisations. For details contact general enquiries: telephone: +44 (0) 1243 771107, fax: +44 (0) 1243 786300 or email: enquiries@summersdale.com.

CONTENTS

EDITOR'S NOTE

A cousin of mine still calls our grandmother 'Banmar' because he couldn't pronounce 'Grandma' correctly when he was a baby. A friend of my mother's is called 'Mango' by her grandchildren. I've heard of Gramma, Mumma, Noni, Nairn and Nan. It doesn't matter what words are used, the meaning is the same. The mother of a parent. Bigger than them; and, of course, anything greater is Grand. So there she is – Grandmother. The great heart and head of the family. The Matriarch.

Of course, all families are different. All families are a little crazy. But if family is the most important thing there is, those of us lucky enough to know the generations before ours must treasure them.

So it doesn't matter if she is known as Nanny or Gran. It doesn't matter whether her house smells of dried lavender or freshly baked cookies. It doesn't matter whether she wears antique pearls or wellington boots. What matters is that we realise how lucky we are to have her wisdom, her guidance, her experience. For she is precious. She is grand. And, Grandma, we love you.

WHAT IS A GRAND- MOTHER?

Something magical happens when parents turn into grandparents.

PAUL LINDEN

*

The simplest toy, one which even the youngest child can operate, is called a grandparent.

SAM LEVENSON

*

The best babysitters, of course, are the baby's grandparents… which is why most grandparents flee to Florida.

DAVE BARRY

MY DAUGHTER POINTED OUT THE OTHER DAY 'A GRANNY IS ONLY A DOUBLE-DECKER MUMMY.'

Jilly Cooper

Nobody can do for little
children what grandparents do.
Grandparents sort of sprinkle
stardust over the lives of
little children.

ALEX HALEY

BEING A GRANDMOTHER IS THE
GREATEST JOY AND THE BEST
JOB I WILL EVER HAVE.

Hillary Clinton

If nothing is going well,
call your grandmother.

ITALIAN PROVERB

*

Grandmother. The true power
behind the power.

LISA BIRNBACH

*

Just about the time a woman
thinks her work is done,
she becomes a grandmother.

EDWARD H. DRESCHNACK

If grandmas hadn't existed,
kids would have inevitably
invented them.

ARTHUR KORNHABER

✳

You make all your mistakes with
your own children so by the time
your grandchildren arrive,
you… get it right.

LIZ FENTON

✳

Grandmothers open the
doors to the future.

HELEN KETCHUM

Most grandmas have a
touch of the scallywag.

HELEN THOMSON

Grandmothers always have time to
talk and make you feel special.

CATHERINE PULSIFER

A grandmother pretends
she doesn't know who you
are on Halloween.

ERMA BOMBECK

A GRANDMA IS WARM HUGS AND SWEET MEMORIES. SHE REMEMBERS ALL OF YOUR ACCOMPLISHMENTS AND FORGETS ALL OF YOUR MISTAKES.

Barbara Cage

They give unconditional love, kindness, patience, humour, comfort, lessons in life. And, most importantly, cookies.

RUDOLPH GIULIANI ON GRANDPARENTS

*

A grandmother is a safe haven.

SUZETTE HADEN ELGIN

*

It is into us that the lives of grandparents have gone.

CHARLES AND ANN MORSE

THE
GRANDCHILD
COMETH!

When a child is born,
so are grandmothers.

JUDITH LEVY

*

Grandmothers hold babies
on their laps under the stars
and whisper in their ears.

RICK BRAGG

*

Children's children are
a crown to the aged.

PROVERBS 17:6

EVERY BABY NEEDS A LAP.

Henry Robin

Grandchildren are
God's way of compensating
us for growing old.

MARY H. WALDRIP

＊

EVERY BABY BORN
INTO THE WORLD IS A FINER
ONE THAN THE LAST.

Charles Dickens

A baby is a blank cheque made payable to the human race.

BARBARA CHRISTINE SEIFERT

AH, BABIES!
THEY'RE MORE THAN
JUST ADORABLE LITTLE
CREATURES ON WHOM YOU
CAN BLAME YOUR FARTS.

Tina Fey

Every baby is a fresh new flower
who can smile, laugh, giggle, dance,
love and sing with mother earth.

DEBASISH MRIDHA

*

Babies are always more trouble than
you thought – and more wonderful.

CHARLES OSGOOD

*

The children we bring into
the world are small replicas of
ourselves… the pride and joy of
grandfathers and grandmothers.

AZELENE WILLIAMS

A baby's a full-time job for three adults.

Erica Jong

Families with babies and families
without are so sorry for each other.

ED HOWE

＊

An hour with your grandchildren
can make you feel young again.
Anything longer than that and you
start to age quickly.

GENE PERRET

＊

You know what the great
thing about babies is? They are
like little bundles of hope.

LISH McBRIDE

BABIES ARE SUCH A NICE WAY TO START PEOPLE.

Don Herold

People who say they sleep like a
baby usually don't have one.

LEO J. BURKE

A baby is a wishing well. Everyone
puts their hopes, their fears,
their pasts, their two cents in.

ELIZABETH BARD

I wish I had the energy that
my grandchildren have –
if only for self-defence.

GENE PERRET

GRANNY
KNOWS
BEST

If we have bikes to ride and
people to love, now is the time.

ELISABETH KÜBLER-ROSS

*

Be equal to your talent, not your age.
At times let the gap between
them be embarrassing.

YEVGENY YEVTUSHENKO

*

We may encounter many defeats,
but we must not be defeated.

MAYA ANGELOU

ATTITUDE IS
A LITTLE THING
THAT MAKES A
BIG DIFFERENCE.

Zig Ziglar

You can't do it all,
all the time, by yourself.

YASMEEN ABDUR-RAHMAN

*

LIFE IS A SHIPWRECK
BUT WE MUST NOT FORGET
TO SING IN THE LIFEBOATS.

Voltaire

Life's under no obligation to
give us what we expect.

MARGARET MITCHELL

Life may not be the party
we hoped for, but while we are here
we might as well dance.

ANONYMOUS

Always be a first-rate version of
yourself, instead of a second-rate
version of somebody else.

JUDY GARLAND

DO GOOD: AS WE HAVE TIME, AND OPPORTUNITY, TO DO GOOD IN EVERY POSSIBLE KIND, AND IN EVERY POSSIBLE DEGREE TO ALL MEN.

John Wesley

If you would be loved,
love and be lovable.

BENJAMIN FRANKLIN

*

Determine to live life
with flair and laughter.

MAYA ANGELOU

*

The pen that writes your life story
must be held in your own hand.

IRENE C. KASSORLA

He who laughs most, learns best.

JOHN CLEESE

How many cares one loses
when one decides not to be
something but to be someone.

COCO CHANEL

The most exhausting thing
in life is being insincere.

ANNE MORROW LINDBERGH

There is just one life for
each of us: our own.

EURIPIDES

Health is real wealth and peace
of mind is real happiness.

SANCHITA PANDEY

A compromise is the art of
dividing a cake in such a way that
everyone believes that he has
got the biggest piece.

PAUL GAUGUIN

LIL'
DARLINGS

Perfect love sometimes does not come until the first grandchild.

WELSH PROVERB

*

Grandparents, like heroes, are as necessary to a child's growth as vitamins.

JOYCE ALLSTON

*

Children are a great comfort in your old age – and they help you reach it faster, too.

LIONEL KAUFFMAN

A GRANDCHILD IS
LIKE A FINE JEWEL
SET IN AN OLD RING.

Anne Lamott

There are only two lasting bequests we can hope to give our children. One of these… is roots, the other, wings.

PROVERB

✳

Grandkids bring you into a sweeter, slower present.

ADAIR LARA

✳

Grandmotherhood initiated me into a world of play, where all things became fresh… and honest again through my grandchildren's eyes.

SUE MONK KIDD

We find delight in the beauty
and happiness of children
that makes the heart
too big for the body.

RALPH WALDO EMERSON

NO MATTER HOW MANY
GRANDCHILDREN YOU MAY
HAVE, EACH ONE HOLDS A
SPECIAL PLACE IN YOUR HEART.

Alvaretta Roberts

Even when freshly washed and
relieved of all obvious confections,
children tend to be sticky.

FRAN LEBOWITZ

*

Grandparents are there to
help the child get into mischief
they haven't thought of yet.

GENE PERRET

*

While we try to teach our
children all about life, our children
teach us what life is all about.

ANGELA SCHWINDT

You can learn many things from children. How much patience you have, for instance.

FRANKLIN P. JONES

Our death is not an end if we can live on in our children.

ALBERT EINSTEIN

Our grandchildren accept us for ourselves, without rebuke or effort to change us.

RUTH GOODE

WHAT IS A HOME WITHOUT CHILDREN? QUIET.

Henny Youngman

By the time the youngest children have learned to keep the house tidy, the oldest grandchildren... tear it to pieces.

CHRISTOPHER MORLEY

IT'S FUNNY THAT THOSE THINGS YOUR KIDS DID THAT GOT ON YOUR NERVES SEEM SO CUTE WHEN YOUR GRANDCHILDREN DO THEM.

Anonymous

FAMILY
MATTERS!

Family is the most important
thing in the world.

DIANA, PRINCESS OF WALES

The only rock I know that stays
steady, the only institution I know
that works, is the family.

LEE IACOCCA

We all take different paths in life, but
no matter where we go, we take a
little of each other everywhere.

TIM McGRAW

Never judge someone by their relatives.

Charles Martin

Grandchildren are the dots
that connect the lines from
generation to generation.

LOIS WYSE

LOVE GROWS MORE TREMENDOUSLY
FULL, SWIFT, POIGNANT,
AS THE YEARS MULTIPLY.

Zane Grey

When you look at your life
the greatest happinesses
are family happinesses.

JOYCE BROTHERS

We cannot destroy kindred:
our chains stretch a little
sometimes, but they never break.

MARQUISE DE SÉVIGNÉ

The informality of family life
is a blessed condition that
allows us… to become our best
while looking our worst.

MARGE KENNEDY

Home is a place not only
of strong affections,
but of entire unreserved;
it is life's undress rehearsal,
its backroom.

HARRIET BEECHER STOWE

*

There is nothing like staying at
home for real comfort.

JANE AUSTEN

*

Family – that dear octopus
from whose tentacles we never
quite escape, nor, in our inmost
hearts, ever quite wish to.

DODIE SMITH

WHERE WE LOVE IS HOME, HOME THAT OUR FEET MAY LEAVE, BUT NOT OUR HEARTS.

Oliver Wendell Holmes Sr

Rejoice with your family in
the beautiful land of life!

ALBERT EINSTEIN

Family faces are magic mirrors.
Looking at people who belong to us,
we see the past, present, and future.

GAIL LUMET BUCKLEY

As we seek to strengthen the
enduring values of the family,
it is appropriate that we
honour our grandparents.

JIMMY CARTER

We often take for granted the very things that most deserve our gratitude.

CYNTHIA OZICK

LOVE IS THE GREATEST GIFT THAT ONE GENERATION CAN LEAVE TO ANOTHER.

Richard Garnett

THE
GOLDEN
YEARS

The old are the precious gem
in the centre of the household.

CHINESE PROVERB

What find you better or
more honourable than age?

SHACKERLEY MARMION

Life, if well lived, is long enough.

SENECA

CHILDHOOD ITSELF IS SCARCELY MORE LOVELY THAN A CHEERFUL, KINDLY, SUNSHINY OLD AGE.

Lydia Maria Child

You live longer once you realise that any time spent being unhappy is wasted.

RUTH E. RENKL

BEING HAPPY IS A REQUISITE FOR LONGEVITY.

Chidi Prosper Agbugba

A good old age can be the
crown of our life's experiences,
the masterwork of a lifetime.

HELEN NEARING

If you want a thing done well,
get a couple of old broads to do it.

BETTE DAVIS

Old women are like ageing
strudels – the crust may not be
so lovely, but the filling has
come at last into its own.

ROBERT FARRAR CAPON

The matron dignity
of Autumn's tread
Can bring with it a joy
more grave and deep.

FANNY CHARLOTTE WYNDHAM MONTGOMERY

Some turn to vinegar,
but the best improve with age.

POPE JOHN XXIII

My goal is to say or do at least
one outrageous thing every week.

MAGGIE KUHN ON OLD AGE

In masks outrageous and austere
The years go by in single file;
But none has merited my fear,
And none has quite
escaped my smile.

ELINOR HOYT WYLIE

Perhaps one has to be very old
before one learns to be amused
rather than shocked.

PEARL S. BUCK

Our latter years can be some
of the most rewarding
and fulfilling of our lives.

PAUL SILWAY

It's a perk of getting old.
You can be annoying and
people just call you eccentric.

LAUREN DANE

The great thing about getting older
is that you don't lose all the
other ages you've been.

MADELEINE L'ENGLE

I believe the true function of
age is memory. I'm recording
as fast as I can.

RITA MAE BROWN

Now that I'm over 60, I'm veering toward respectability.

SHELLEY WINTERS

*

Age does not diminish the extreme disappointment of having a scoop of ice cream fall from the cone.

JIM FIEBIG

*

I think you should grow old gracefully in public – and disgracefully in private.

JERRY HALL

CROWNED
IN SILVER

Grey hair is the glory of a long life.
LAILAH GIFTY AKITA

*

The easiest way to diminish the
appearance of wrinkles is to
keep your glasses off
when you look in the mirror.
JOAN RIVERS

*

You can take no credit
for beauty at sixteen.
But if you are beautiful at sixty,
it will be your soul's own doing.
MARIE STOPES

Beauty is not in
the face; beauty is a
light in the heart.

Kahlil Gibran

Grey locks –
Nature's flag of truce.

JAMES LENDALL BASFORD

TIME IS A DRESSMAKER
SPECIALISING IN ALTERATIONS.

Faith Baldwin

Grey hairs seem to my fancy like
the soft light of the moon,
silvering over the evening of life.

JEAN PAUL RICHTER

Character contributes to
beauty. It fortifies a woman
as her youth fades.

JACQUELINE BISSET

She was gracious and yet fading,
like an old statue in a garden,
that symbolises the weather…
it has endured.

DJUNA BARNES

Taking joy in living is a
woman's best cosmetic.

ROSALIND RUSSELL

Time is a great healer,
but a poor beautician.

LUCILLE S. HARPER

There is no cosmetic for
beauty like happiness.

MARGUERITE GARDINER

Cheerfulness and contentment
are great beautifiers,
and are fatuous preservers
of youthful looks.

CHARLES DICKENS

When you have loved as she has
loved, you grow old beautifully.

W. SOMERSET MAUGHAM

Let us respect grey hairs,
especially our own.

J. P. SEARS

I think your whole life shows in your
face and you should be proud of that.

LAUREN BACALL

*

I refuse to think of them
as chin hairs. I think of them
as stray eyebrows.

JANETTE BARBER

*

She looked like
autumn, when leaves turned
and fruit ripened.

SARAH ADDISON ALLEN

A BEAUTIFUL LADY IS AN ACCIDENT OF NATURE. A BEAUTIFUL OLD LADY IS A WORK OF ART.

Louis Nizer

Varicose veins are the result of an improper selection of grandparents.

WILLIAM OSLER

You can say what you like about long dresses, but they cover a multitude of shins.

MAE WEST

Youth and beauty are not accomplishments, they're the temporary happy by-products of time and/ or DNA. Don't hold your breath for either.

CARRIE FISHER

YOUNG AT HEART

It takes a long time to become young.

PABLO PICASSO

*

When it comes to staying young,
a mind-lift beats a face-lift any day.

MARTY BUCELLA

*

The secret of staying young is to
live honestly, eat slowly,
and lie about your age.

LUCILLE BALL

IN A DREAM YOU ARE NEVER EIGHTY.

Anne Sexton

If you carry your childhood with you, you never become older.

TOM STOPPARD

THE TRAGEDY OF OLD AGE IS
NOT THAT ONE IS OLD,
BUT THAT ONE IS YOUNG.

Oscar Wilde

I will never give in to old age
until I become old.
And I'm not old yet!

TINA TURNER

*

Old age is fifteen years
older than I am.

BERNARD BARUCH

*

Inside every older person
is a younger person wondering
what happened.

JENNIFER YANE

I'm not denying my age,
I'm embellishing my youth.

TAMARA REYNOLDS

We are always the same age inside.

GERTRUDE STEIN

Growing old is mandatory;
growing up is optional.

CHILI DAVIS

Everyone is the age of their heart.
GUATEMALAN PROVERB

You can be glamorous at any age.
JOAN COLLINS

It is the rudest word in my dictionary,
'retire'. And 'old' is another one…
I like 'enthusiastic'.
JUDI DENCH

There are days of oldness,
and then one gets young again.
It goes backward and forward,
not in one direction.

KATHARINE BUTLER HATHAWAY

The idea is to die young
as late as possible.

ASHLEY MONTAGU

It's not that age brings
childhood back again,
age merely shows what
children we remain.

JOHANN WOLFGANG VON GOETHE

I waltz while I wait for the kettle to boil. This pleasure is for the old who live alone.

FLORIDA SCOTT-MAXWELL

THE TRICK IS GROWING UP WITHOUT GROWING OLD.

Casey Stengel

LET'S
CELEBRATE!

THERE IS STILL NO CURE FOR THE COMMON BIRTHDAY.

John Glenn

Celebration has many different outfits but she always wears the same beautiful dancing shoes.

MARY ANNE RADMACHER

Birthdays are good for you. Statistics show that the people who have the most live the longest.

Larry Lorenzoni

Uncles and aunts, and cousins,
are all very well… but a grandmother,
at holiday time, is worth them all.

FANNY FERN

*

The way I see it, you should live
every day like it's your birthday.

PARIS HILTON

*

You know you're getting old when
the candles cost more than the cake.

BOB HOPE

The first fact about the celebration of
a birthday is that it is a good
way of affirming defiantly, and
even flamboyantly, that it is
a good thing to be alive.

G. K. CHESTERTON

Birthdays are nature's way of
telling you to eat more cake.

JO BRAND

Calories don't count if they're
connected to a celebration.
Everyone knows this.

JANET EVANOVICH

It is lovely, when I forget all birthdays, including my own, to find that somebody remembers me.

ELLEN GLASGOW

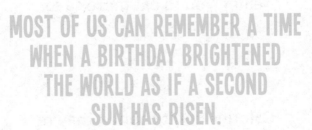

MOST OF US CAN REMEMBER A TIME WHEN A BIRTHDAY BRIGHTENED THE WORLD AS IF A SECOND SUN HAS RISEN.

Robert Staughton Lynd

Let us celebrate the occasion
with wine and sweet words.

PLAUTUS

*

My birthday! What a different sound
that word had in my youthful ear.

MALCOLM FORBES

*

Last year my birthday cake
looked like a prairie fire.

RODNEY DANGERFIELD

Our birthdays are feathers in
the broad wing of time.

JEAN PAUL RICHTER

TO BE SEVENTY YEARS YOUNG
IS SOMETIMES FAR MORE CHEERFUL
AND HOPEFUL THAN TO BE
FORTY YEARS OLD.

Oliver Wendell Holmes Sr

THE BEST BIRTHDAYS OF ALL
ARE THOSE THAT HAVEN'T
ARRIVED YET.

Robert Orben

GRANNY'S
KITCHEN

If God had intended us
to follow recipes,
He wouldn't have given
us grandmothers.

LINDA HENLEY

[Grandma's] kitchen, without doubt,
was the center of creation,
all things revolved about it.

RAY BRADBURY

The tradition of Italian cooking
is that of the matriarch.
This is the cooking of grandma.

MARIO BATALI

THE ADVANTAGE OF LEARNING AT GRANDMOTHER'S ELBOW IS DISCOVERING THINGS WHICH ARE NOT FOUND IN ANY BOOK.

Frederick Douglass Opie

It is in an old kitchen that
the best food is made.

FRENCH PROVERB

MY MOM SAID THE TWO MOST
IMPORTANT KITCHEN UTENSILS
ARE ATTACHED TO YOUR ARMS.

Rachael Ray

If baking is any labour at all,
it's a labour of love…
that gets passed from
generation to generation.

REGINA BRETT

*

There's something special about
a grandmother's house.
You never forget how it smells.

FREDRIK BACKMAN

*

I loved their home. Everything
smelled older, worn but safe;
the food aroma had baked itself
into the furniture.

SUSAN STRASBERG ON HER GRANDPARENTS' HOME

A kitchen is a good place to be,
almost always the best place
in the house.

MICHAEL RUHLMAN

*

And, indeed, is there not something
holy about a great kitchen?

ANGELA CARTER

*

When men reach their sixties
and retire, they go to pieces.
Women go right on cooking.

GAIL SHEEHY

My mother's menu
consisted of two choices:
take it or leave it.

Buddy Hackett

Even at her most solitary, a cook
in the kitchen is surrounded by
generations of cooks past.

LAURIE COLWIN

❋

Don't eat anything your
great-great-great grandmother
wouldn't recognise as food.

MICHAEL POLLAN

❋

Here, he knew by certain
instinct, was a woman who made
wonderful cookies and
would give you some.

CHARLOTTE MacLEOD

Cookies are made with
butter and love.

NORWEGIAN PROVERB

A balanced diet is a cookie
in each hand.

BARBARA JOHNSON

To feel safe and warm
on a cold wet night,
all you really need is soup.

LAURIE COLWIN

The kitchen is a country in which
there are always
discoveries to be made.

GRIMOD DE LA REYNIÈRE

*

The older I get the more
I become an apple pie,
sparkling cider kind of guy.

SCOTT FOLEY

*

Happiness is
baking cookies. Happiness is
giving them away.

MAIDA HEATTER

GRANNY'S
GARDEN

Everyone, without regard to type,
acquires grey hairs and philosophies
of life. Many also acquire gardens.

JANICE EMILY BOWERS

＊

Remember that children, marriages,
and flower gardens reflect
the kind of care they get.

H. JACKSON BROWN JR

＊

Maturity can always be depended
on. Ripeness can be trusted.

OSCAR WILDE

TO PLANT A GARDEN IS TO BELIEVE IN TOMORROW.

Audrey Hepburn

Happiness will grow if you plant the seeds of love in the garden of hope with compassion and care.

DEBASISH MRIDHA

KIND HEARTS ARE THE GARDENS,
KIND THOUGHTS ARE THE ROOTS,
KIND WORDS ARE THE FLOWERS,
KIND DEEDS ARE THE FRUITS,
TAKE CARE OF YOUR GARDEN...

Henry Wadsworth Longfellow

Gardening is an
instrument of grace.

MAY SARTON

Green fingers
are the extension of a
verdant heart.

RUSSELL PAGE

Gardens are
a form of
autobiography.

SYDNEY EDDISON

The philosopher who said that
work well done never needs doing
over… never weeded a garden.

RAY D. EVERSON

It's difficult to think anything but
pleasant thoughts while eating
a homegrown tomato.

LEWIS GRIZZARD

I want death to find me
planting my cabbages.

MICHEL DE MONTAIGNE

He who plants a tree
plants a hope.

LUCY LARCOM

*

Trees and plants always look like the
people they live with, somehow.

ZORA NEALE HURSTON

*

If I had a single flower
for every time I think of you,
I could walk forever in my garden.

CLAUDIA ADRIENNE GRANDI

A GARDEN IS WHERE YOU CAN FIND A WHOLE SPECTRUM OF LIFE, BIRTH AND DEATH.

Tiffany Baker

Wherever you go,
no matter what the weather,
always bring your own sunshine.

ANTHONY J. D'ANGELO

AND ADD TO THESE RETIRED
LEISURE, THAT IN TRIM GARDENS
TAKES HIS PLEASURE.

John Milton

A garden is never so good
as it will be next year.

THOMAS COOPER

*

If you look the right way,
you can see that the
whole world is a garden.

FRANCES HODGSON BURNETT

*

In search of my mother's
garden, I found my own.

ALICE WALKER

FEELING
CREAKY?

I do wish I could tell you my
age but it's impossible.
It keeps changing all the time.

GREER GARSON

Life is one long process
of getting tired.

SAMUEL BUTLER

Nature does not equally distribute
energy. Some people are born
old and tired while others are
going strong at seventy.

DOROTHY THOMPSON

I'M AT THAT AGE WHERE EVERYTHING MOTHER NATURE GAVE ME, FATHER TIME IS TAKING AWAY.

Anonymous

I fear vastly more a futile, incompetent old age than I do any form of death.

WILLIAM ALLEN WHITE

I CAN LIE CONVINCINGLY ABOUT MY AGE BECAUSE AT MY AGE I CAN'T ALWAYS REMEMBER WHAT IT IS.

Violet Conti

Getting older comes with abilities.
Being old comes with disabilities.

MOKOKOMA MOKHONOANA

The really frightening thing about
middle age is the knowledge
that you'll grow out of it.

DORIS DAY

In youth we run into difficulties.
In old age difficulties run into us.

BEVERLY SILLS

Never lose sight of the fact that
old age needs so little but needs
that little so much.

MARGARET WILLOUR

*

As we advance in life the circle
of our pains enlarges, while that
of our pleasures contracts.

MADAME SWETCHINE

*

As we grow older, our capacity
for enjoyment shrinks,
but not our appetite for it.

MIGNON McLAUGHLIN

Years may wrinkle the skin,
but to give up enthusiasm
wrinkles the soul.

SAMUEL ULLMAN

*

I ADVISE YOU TO GO ON LIVING
SOLELY TO ENRAGE THOSE WHO
ARE PAYING YOUR ANNUITIES. IT IS
THE ONLY PLEASURE I HAVE LEFT.

Voltaire

Everything slows down with age, except the time it takes cake and ice cream to reach your hips.

John M. Wagner

Once I realised how expensive
funerals are, I began to exercise
and watch my diet.

THOMAS SOWELL

*

An older friend consoled me.
'Don't complain about growing old –
many, many people do not
have that privilege.'

EARL WARREN

*

Be careful about
reading health books.
You may die of a misprint.

MARK TWAIN

I've often thought that the ageing
process could be slowed down
if it had to work its way
through Parliament.

EDWINA CURRIE

＊

Time has laid his hand
Upon my heart, gently, not smiting it,
But as a harper lays his open palm
Upon his harp,
to deaden its vibrations.

HENRY WADSWORTH LONGFELLOW

＊

What's remarkable… is not that we
wear out but that we last
so long in the grip of gravity.

SCOTT RUSSELL SANDERS ON OLD AGE

A WRINKLE
IN TIME

Wrinkles should merely indicate
where smiles have been.

MARK TWAIN

❋

When grace is joined with wrinkles,
it is adorable. There is an
unspeakable dawn in happy old age.

VICTOR HUGO

❋

As we grow old,
the beauty steals inward.

RALPH WALDO EMERSON

WE DID NOT CHANGE AS WE GREW OLDER; WE JUST BECAME MORE CLEARLY OURSELVES.

Lynn Hall

The criterion of true beauty is,
that it increases on examination;
of false, that it lessens.

GEORGE GRENVILLE

HOW PLEASANT IS THE DAY WHEN
WE GIVE UP STRIVING TO BE
YOUNG OR SLENDER.

William James

It is sad to grow old
but nice to ripen.

BRIGITTE BARDOT

＊

Her grandmother, as she gets older,
is not fading but rather
becoming more concentrated.

PAULETTE BATES ALDEN

＊

To me, fair friend,
you never can be old,
For as you were when
first your eye I eyed,
Such seems your beauty still.

WILLIAM SHAKESPEARE

Beautiful is old age –
beautiful as the slow-dropping
mellow autumn of
a rich glorious summer.

J. A. FROUDE

❋

I AM LUMINOUS WITH AGE.

Meridel LeSueur

You can only perceive real beauty
in a person as they get older.

ANOUK AIMÉE

NO SPRING
NOR SUMMER BEAUTY
HATH SUCH GRACEAS I HAVE SEEN
IN ONE AUTUMNAL FACE.

John Donne

Every wrinkle [is] but a
notch in the quiet calendar
of a well-spent life.

CHARLES DICKENS

WOMEN ARE BEAUTIFUL
BECAUSE THEIR FACES SHOW
THAT THEY KNOW THEY HAVE
LOST SOMETHING AND PICKED
UP SOMETHING ELSE.

Henry Rollins

Time, which changes people, does not alter the image we have retained of them.

Marcel Proust

WISDOM OF THE AGED

Wisdom doesn't necessarily come with age. Sometimes age just shows up all by itself.

TOM WILSON

*

Retire from work,
but not from life.

M. K. SONI

*

To keep the heart unwrinkled,
to be hopeful, kindly,
cheerful, reverent – that is
to triumph over old age.

THOMAS BAILEY ALDRICH

The key to
successful ageing is...
to pay as little attention
to it as possible.

Judith Regan

That which seems the height of absurdity in one generation often becomes the height of wisdom in another.

ADLAI E. STEVENSON

＊

AGE AND YOUTH LOOK UPON LIFE
FROM THE OPPOSITE ENDS
OF THE TELESCOPE;
IT IS EXCEEDINGLY LONG,
IT IS EXCEEDINGLY SHORT.

Henry Ward Beecher

Old age lives minutes slowly,
hours quickly;
childhood chews hours
and swallows minutes.

MALCOLM DE CHAZAL

＊

In youth the days are short and
the years are long; in old age the
years are short and the
days are long.

NIKITA IVANOVICH PANIN

＊

In youth study;
in maturity compose;
in old age correct.

WILLIAM BENTON CLULOW

Winter is dead; spring is crazy;
summer is cheerful
and autumn is wise!

MEHMET MURAT ILDAN

＊

You are never too old to set another
goal or to dream a new dream.

LES BROWN

＊

May I govern my passion
with an absolute sway,
And grow wiser and better as
my strength wears away,
Without gout or stone,
by a gentle decay.

WALTER POPE

When one has reached
eighty-one one likes to sit back
and let the world turn by itself.

SEÁN O'CASEY

I think of life itself now
as a wonderful play that I've
written for myself.

SHIRLEY MacLAINE

Minds ripen at very
different ages.

ELIZABETH MONTAGU

THE OLDER YOU GET
THE LOUDER YOU
SHOULD SING.

Judi Dench

You are as young as your faith,
as old as your doubt;
as young as your self-confidence,
as old as your fear;
as young as your hope,
as old as your despair.

SAMUEL ULLMAN

LIFE IS THE SUM OF ALL
YOUR CHOICES.

Albert Camus

Anyone can get old. All you have
to do is to live long enough.

GROUCHO MARX

✳

By plucking her petals,
you do not gather
the beauty of the flower.

RABINDRANATH TAGORE

✳

In three words I can
sum up everything I've learned
about life – it goes on.

ROBERT FROST

THE GOOD
OLD DAYS

My granny used to say if you're too sharp you'll cut yourself.

TERRY PRATCHETT

＊

My grandmother has a bumper sticker on her car that says, 'Sexy Senior Citizen'.

ANDY ROONEY

＊

My grandma showed me that there is always something to learn, that everybody got something to tell you.

KATHLEEN GRISSOM

IT IS, I SUPPOSE, THE BUSINESS OF GRANDPARENTS TO CREATE MEMORIES AND THE RELATIVE OF MEMORIES: TRADITIONS.

Ellen Goodman

My grandmother was a
Jewish juggler: she used to worry
about six things at once.

RICHARD LEWIS

*

MY GRANDMOTHER WOULD SAY,
'MAKE SURE YOU REMAIN THAT
SOUTHERN GENTLEMAN THAT
I'VE TAUGHT YOU TO BE.'

Jamie Foxx

Regrets are the natural
property of grey hairs.

CHARLES DICKENS

How far away the stars
seem, and how far
Is our first kiss, and ah,
how old my heart!

WILLIAM BUTLER YEATS

Nostalgia is a file that removes the
rough edges from the good old days.

DOUG LARSON

My grandmother's 90;
she's dating a man 93.
They never argue:
they can't hear each other.

CATHY LADMAN

✳

She was… a very humble person
and a very plain-spoken person.
She was one of those quiet heroes.

BARACK OBAMA ABOUT HIS GRANDMOTHER

✳

My grandmother was a very tough
woman. She buried three husbands
and two of them were just napping.

RITA RUDNER

Piety and peace made old age lovely, and the mere presence of this tranquil soul seemed to fill the room with a reposeful charm none could resist.

LOUISA MAY ALCOTT

THE LEAVES OF MEMORY
SEEMED TO MAKE
A MOURNFUL RUSTLING
IN THE DARK.

Henry Wadsworth Longfellow

My old mam reads the
obituary page every day but she
could never understand
how people always die in
alphabetical order.

FRANK CARSON

A WONDERFUL WOMAN MY
GRANDMOTHER, 86 YEARS OLD AND
NOT A SINGLE GREY HAIR ON HER
HEAD. SHE'S COMPLETELY BALD.

Les Dawson

As a child I knew almost nothing,
nothing beyond what I had picked
up in my grandmother's house.

V. S. NAIPAUL

✳

Grandma Hutto's flower garden was
a bright patchwork quilt thrown
down inside the pickets.

MARJORIE KINNAN RAWLINGS

✳

You remember someone said that
God gave us memory so that we
might have roses in December.

J. M. BARRIE

GRANNY
LIKES A
DRINK

My grandmother is over eighty
and still doesn't need glasses.
Drinks right out of the bottle.

HENNY YOUNGMAN

*

Health – what my friends are always
drinking to before they fall down.

PHYLLIS DILLER

*

Alcohol is the anaesthesia by which
we endure the operation of life.

GEORGE BERNARD SHAW

Always do sober what you said you'd do drunk. That will teach you to keep your mouth shut.

Ernest Hemingway

Drink… does wash away cares,
and stirs the mind to its depths.

SENECA

*

There is nothing for a case of
nerves like a case of beer.

JOAN GOLDSTEIN

*

I like to have a martini,
Two at the very most.
After three I'm under the table,
After four I'm under my host.

DOROTHY PARKER

WHERE DRUNKENNESS REIGNS, THERE REASON IS AN EXILE.

Francis Quarles

Wine leads to folly, making even the wise to laugh immoderately, to dance, and to utter what had better have been kept silent.

HOMER

ALCOHOL IS A MISUNDERSTOOD VITAMIN.

P. G. Wodehouse

No animal ever invented
anything so bad as drunkenness –
or so good as drink.

G. K. CHESTERTON

*

Drunkenness is
the vice of a good constitution
or of a bad memory.

CHARLES CALEB COLTON

*

The heart which Grief
hath canker'd
Hath one unfailing remedy
– the Tankard.

CHARLES STUART CALVERLEY

FEW THINGS
SURPASS OLD WINE.

Lord Byron

I have been advised by the
best medical authority, at my age,
not to attempt to give up alcohol.

W. C. FIELDS

*

Wine improves with age.
I improve with wine.

ANONYMOUS

*

Almost anything can be
preserved in alcohol, except
health, happiness, and money.

MARY WILSON LITTLE

Wine makes a poor man
rich in imagination,
a rich man poor in reality.

EDWARD PARSONS DAY

*

DRINK TO-DAY,
AND DROWN ALL SORROW;
YOU SHALL PERHAPS
NOT DO IT TO-MORROW:
BEST, WHILE YOU HAVE IT,
USE YOUR BREATH;
THERE IS NO DRINKING
AFTER DEATH.

Francis Beaumont and John Fletcher

STILL
GOT IT!

If youth only knew and
age only could.

ROBERT LOUIS STEVENSON

*

You know you're getting
old when a four-letter word for
something pleasurable two
people can do in bed is R-E-A-D.

DENIS NORDEN

*

Nothing makes people crosser than
being considered too old for love.

NANCY MITFORD

**A fiddle that's old
is more in tune.**

Sandy Wilson

Age does not protect you
from love. But love, to some
extent, protects you from age.

JEANNE MOREAU

TO SEE AN OLD COUPLE
LOVING EACH OTHER
IS THE BEST SIGHT OF ALL.

William Makepeace Thackeray

Like a prune, you are not getting
any better looking, but you
are getting sweeter.

N. D. STICE

The older one grows,
the more one likes indecency.

VIRGINIA WOOLF

Before we make love
my husband takes a painkiller.

JOAN RIVERS

An archaeologist is the best husband a woman can have. The older she gets the more interested he is in her.

AGATHA CHRISTIE

Those who love deeply never grow old; they may die of old age, but they die young.

ARTHUR WING PINERO

When did my wild oats turn to prunes and all-bran?

LUCY PARKER

Don't worry about avoiding
temptation – as you grow older,
it starts avoiding you.

MICHAEL FORD

One of the best parts of growing
older? You can flirt all you like
since you've become harmless.

LIZ SMITH

Sex appeal is in your heart and head.
I'll be sexy no matter how old
or how my body changes.

SONIA BRAGA

If you can't have fun as
an ageing sex symbol…
I don't know what
will become of you.

RAQUEL WELCH

I'VE STILL GOT FABULOUS
LEGS AND WEAR MINI-SKIRTS.
I'LL KEEP WEARING BIKINIS
TILL I'M 80.

Jerry Hall

MEMENTO
MORI

Gather ye rose-buds while ye may,
Old Time is still a-flying;
And this same flower
that smiles today
Tomorrow will be dying.

ROBERT HERRICK

*

My comfort is, that old age,
that ill-layer-up of beauty, can do
no more spoil upon my face.

WILLIAM SHAKESPEARE

*

I am now old enough to no longer
have a fear of dying young.

BRUCE ADES

THERE IS NO CURE FOR BIRTH AND DEATH, SAVE TO ENJOY THE INTERVAL.

George Santayana

Your time is limited,
so don't waste it
living someone else's life.

STEVE JOBS

*

I LOOK AT THE OBITUARY
PAGE. IF MY NAME IS NOT
ON IT, I GET UP.

Harry Hershfield on his morning routine

Dying is a very dull, dreary affair...
my advice to you is to have
nothing whatever to do with it.

W. SOMERSET MAUGHAM

I'm not afraid of death.
It's the stake one puts up in order
to play the game of life.

JEAN GIRAUDOUX

I postpone death by living,
by suffering, by error, by risking,
by giving, by losing.

ANAÏS NIN

Death is not the end. There remains
the litigation over the estate.

AMBROSE BIERCE

Memorial services are the
cocktail parties of the geriatric set.

HAROLD MACMILLAN

Old age is… a lot of crossed off
names in an address book.

RONALD BLYTHE

Old age is creeping on apace,
And clouds come o'er
the sunset of our day.

LORD BYRON

I shall not die of a cold…
I shall die of having lived.

WILLA CATHER

Are we not better and at home
In dreamful autumn…?

ERNEST DOWSON

An old age serene and bright,
And lovely as a Lapland night,
Shall lead thee to thy grave.

WILLIAM WORDSWORTH

YEARS FOLLOWING YEARS STEAL
SOMETHING EVERY DAY;
AT LAST THEY STEAL US
FROM OURSELVES AWAY.

Horace ·

AGE IS OPPORTUNITY NO LESS THAN YOUTH ITSELF, THOUGH IN ANOTHER DRESS, AND AS THE EVENING TWILIGHT FADES AWAY THE SKY IS FILLED WITH STARS, INVISIBLE BY DAY.

Henry Wadsworth Longfellow

That it will never come again
Is what makes life so sweet.

EMILY DICKINSON

LIFE DOES NOT CEASE TO BE
FUNNY WHEN PEOPLE DIE
ANY MORE THAN IT CEASES TO BE
SERIOUS WHEN PEOPLE LAUGH.

George Bernard Shaw

YOUTH
OF
TODAY

The youth of the present day
are quite monstrous. They have
absolutely no respect for dyed hair.

OSCAR WILDE

Youth is the most beautiful thing
in this world… what a pity that it
has to be wasted on children!

GEORGE BERNARD SHAW

There is nothing wrong with the
younger generation which the older
generation did not outgrow.

ANONYMOUS

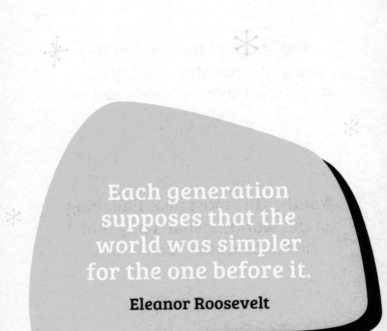

Each generation
supposes that the
world was simpler
for the one before it.

Eleanor Roosevelt

In old age, we are better able to prevent misfortunes from coming, and in youth better able to bear them when they come.

ARTHUR SCHOPENHAUER

*

YOUTH WOULD BE AN IDEAL STATE IF IT CAME A LITTLE LATER IN LIFE.

H.H. Asquith

The problem with today's youth is
not being a part of it anymore.

SALVADOR DALÍ

Enjoy your youth. You'll
never be younger than you are
at this very moment.

CHAD SUGG

Youth is a disease from
which we all recover.

DOROTHY FULDHEIM

Life hasn't much to offer except youth, and I suppose for older people, the love of youth in others.

F. SCOTT FITZGERALD

All sorts of allowances are made for the illusions of youth; and none... for the disenchantments of age.

ROBERT LOUIS STEVENSON

To an adolescent, there is nothing in the world more embarrassing than a parent.

DAVE BARRY

ADOLESCENCE: A STAGE
BETWEEN INFANCY
AND ADULTERY.

Ambrose Bierce

To get back my youth I would do anything in the world, except take exercise, get up early, or be respectable.

OSCAR WILDE

IT WOULD BE A GOOD THING IF YOUNG PEOPLE WERE WISE, AND OLD PEOPLE WERE STRONG, BUT GOD HAS ARRANGED THINGS BETTER.

Martin Luther

The denunciation of the young
is a necessary part of the hygiene
of older people, and greatly assists
in the circulation of their blood.

LOGAN PEARSALL SMITH

Age is foolish and forgetful when
it underestimates youth.

J. K. ROWLING

People who don't cherish their
elderly have forgotten whence
they came and whither they go.

RAMSEY CLARK

Heredity is what sets the parents
of a teenager wondering
about each other.

LAURENCE J. PETER

Old people have one advantage
compared with young ones. They
have been young themselves, and
young people haven't been old.

LORD LONGFORD

Snow and adolescence are the
only problems that disappear if
you ignore them long enough.

EARL WILSON

Old age is ready to undertake tasks that youth shirked because they would take too long.

W. SOMERSET MAUGHAM

FEW THINGS ARE MORE SATISFYING THAN SEEING YOUR CHILDREN HAVE TEENAGERS OF THEIR OWN.

Doug Larson

IT WASN'T LIKE THAT IN MY DAY...

We live in an age when pizza gets to your home before the police.

JEFF MARDER

The people who live in a golden age usually go around complaining how yellow everything looks.

RANDALL JARRELL

You can judge your age by the amount of pain you feel when you come in contact with a new idea.

JOHN NUVEEN

TRUTH IS, I WOULDN'T KNOW A GIGABYTE FROM A SNAKEBITE.

Dolly Parton

In my day, a juvenile delinquent
was a kid who owed tuppence
on an overdue library book.

MAX BYGRAVES

IT WAS NOT SO LONG AGO
THAT PEOPLE THOUGHT
SEMICONDUCTORS WERE
PART-TIME ORCHESTRA LEADERS.

Geraldine Ferraro

Progress may have been all right once, but it went on too long.

OGDEN NASH

The future, like everything else, is no longer quite what it used to be.

PAUL VALÉRY

My nan said, 'What do you mean
when you say the computer
went down on you?'

JOSEPH LONGTHORNE

In my day, we didn't have self-
esteem, we had self-respect, and
no more of it than we had earned.

JANE HADDAM

The older you get the
stronger the wind gets –
and it's always in your face.

JACK NICKLAUS

To exist is to change,
to change is to mature,
to mature is to go on creating
oneself endlessly.

HENRI BERGSON

I CAN REMEMBER WHEN THE AIR
WAS CLEAN AND SEX WAS DIRTY.

George Burns

To err is human, to really foul things up requires a computer.

BILL VAUGHAN

If you assume that the new… is always… better than the old, chances are you've never known anything valuable.

CRISS JAMI

Just because everything is different doesn't mean anything has changed.

IRENE PETER

GRANDMA
IS THE
BEST!

Some of the world's best
educators are grandparents.
CHARLES W. SHEDD

'You're old, Nanny,' said my grandson,
Tom, 'but only on the outside.'
ELLEN TATE

I didn't get old on purpose,
it just happened. If you're lucky,
it could happen to you.
ANDY ROONEY

A family with an old person has a living treasure of gold.

Chinese proverb

My age is as a lusty winter,
frosty but kindly.

WILLIAM SHAKESPEARE

ONE OF LIFE'S GREATEST
MYSTERIES IS HOW THE BOY
WHO WASN'T GOOD ENOUGH TO
MARRY YOUR DAUGHTER CAN BE
THE FATHER OF THE SMARTEST
GRANDCHILD IN THE WORLD.

Jewish proverb

You are the sun, grandma,
you are the sun in my life.

KITTY TSUI

I know what it is… to be brought
up with unconditional love.
In my life that came from
my grandmother.

ANDRÉ LEON TALLEY

We should all have one person
who knows how to bless us…
Grandmother was that person to me.

PHYLLIS GRISSIM-THEROUX

Grandchildren make you feel
great about life, and yourself,
and your ability to love
someone unconditionally.

ANNE LAMOTT

Being grandparents sufficiently
removes us from the responsibilities
so that we can be friends.

ALLAN FROME

When I go to the beach,
my grandchildren try to make
words out of the veins in my legs.

PHYLLIS DILLER

THIS IS A GRANDCHILD'S ULTIMATE PRIVILEGE: KNOWING THAT SOMEONE IS ON YOUR SIDE, ALWAYS.

Fredrik Backman

I don't intentionally spoil
my grandkids. It's just that
correcting them often takes
more energy than I have left.

GENE PERRET

When it seems the world can't
understand, your grandmother's
there to hold your hand.

JOYCE K. ALLEN LOGAN

To become a grandparent is to enjoy
one of the few pleasures in life
for which the consequences
have already been paid.

ROBERT BRAULT

SURELY, TWO OF THE MOST SATISFYING EXPERIENCES IN LIFE MUST BE THOSE OF BEING A GRANDCHILD OR A GRANDPARENT.

Donald A. Norberg

GRANDAD'S
WIT AND WISDOM

QUIPS AND QUOTES FOR GLORIOUS GRANDPAS

RICHARD BENSON

GRANDAD'S WIT AND WISDOM
Quips and Quotes for Glorious Grandpas

Richard Benson

ISBN: 978-1-78685-062-1

Hardback

£9.99

When your roses have been trampled by little feet and the golf has been hijacked by children's TV, reach for this hilarious book, crammed full of quips and quotes to remind you why being a grandad is one of the best jobs in the world.

'Never have children, only grandchildren.'
GORE VIDAL

OLD GIT
WIT AND WISDOM
QUIPS AND QUOTES FOR THE YOUNG AT HEART

RICHARD BENSON